SCIENCE ALLIA

Nick navigates Natural Disasters!

by Carole Marsh

Gallopade is proud to be a member of these educational organizations and associations.

National Science Teachers Association
The National School Supply and Equipment Association
The National Council for the Social Studies
American Booksellers Association
American Library Association

International Reading Association
National Association for Gifted Children
Museum Store Association
Association of Partners for Public Lands
Association of Booksellers for Children

Managing Editor: Sherry Moss
Assistant Editor: Gabrielle Humphrey
Senior Editor: Janice Baker
Cover Design: Vicki DeJoy
Content Design: Yvonne Ford

Other Books In The Series

- **Molly Attracts Opposites with Magnetism!**
- **Ellie Gets Charged About Electricity!**
- **Lara Looks at Light and Color!**
- **Steven Soars into Space Science!**
- **Eddie Explores Ecosystems and the Food Chain!**
- **Willie Gets Wild About Weather!**
- **Mandy Mixes It Up with States of Matter! Solids! Liquids! Gases!**
- **Robby Unearths Rocks and Minerals!**
- **Fred Investigates Force and Motion! Includes Simple Machines**
- **Hannah Hunts for Habitats!**
- **Gina Discovers Genetics, Characteristics and DNA!**
- **Luke Surveys Landforms!**
- **Sam Tunes In to the Science of Sound!**
- **Christina Examines Plant Cells and Animal Cells!**
- **Nina Learns to Appreciate Natural Resources and Conservation!**

Table of Contents

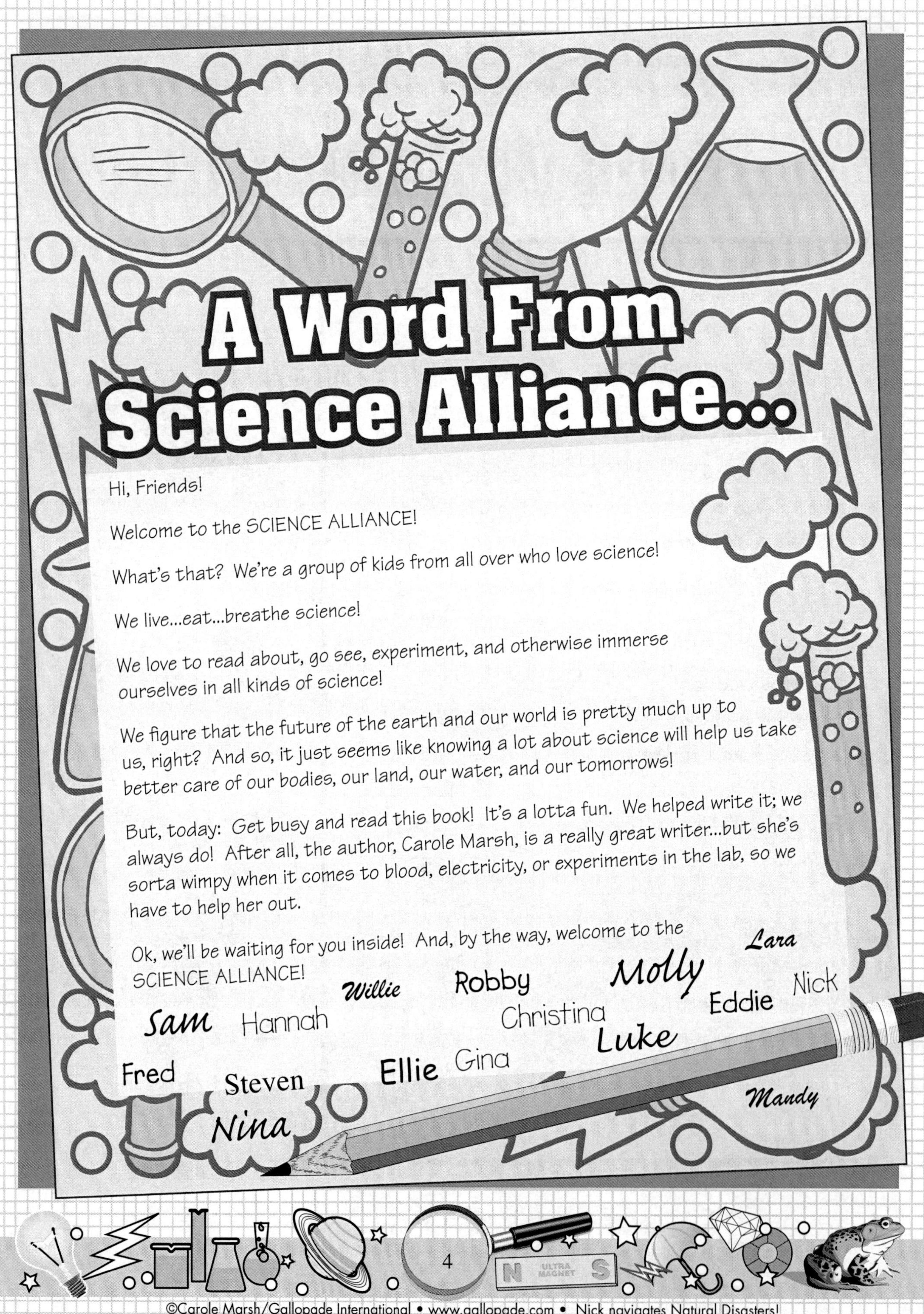

A Word From Science Alliance...

Hi, Friends!

Welcome to the SCIENCE ALLIANCE!

What's that? We're a group of kids from all over who love science!

We live...eat...breathe science!

We love to read about, go see, experiment, and otherwise immerse ourselves in all kinds of science!

We figure that the future of the earth and our world is pretty much up to us, right? And so, it just seems like knowing a lot about science will help us take better care of our bodies, our land, our water, and our tomorrows!

But, today: Get busy and read this book! It's a lotta fun. We helped write it; we always do! After all, the author, Carole Marsh, is a really great writer...but she's sorta wimpy when it comes to blood, electricity, or experiments in the lab, so we have to help her out.

Ok, we'll be waiting for you inside! And, by the way, welcome to the SCIENCE ALLIANCE!

Lara
Willie
Robby
Molly
Nick
Eddie
Sam
Hannah
Christina
Luke
Fred
Steven
Ellie
Gina
Mandy
Nina

A Word From ...
Carole Marsh

Ok, here's the Real Deal:

SCIENCE is fascinating, fun, wild, crazy, easy, hard, mind-blowing, (sometimes lab-blowing!)—and, ESSENTIAL!

In school, you learn to read, you learn to write, and you learn to add and subtract. Those are essential skills! You also learn about the past as you study history and geography.

Science is about the future! And the present! It affects your life each and every minute of each and every day. It always will. It does not matter if you plan to grow up and become a teacher, doctor, lawyer, computer analyst, or anything else—you still MUST know a lot about science.

Science is biology and electricity and windmills and oil deep in the earth and the aurora borealis (Northern Lights) blazing in the sky. Science keeps us warm or makes us cold. It makes our lives easier and better—or, exceedingly miserable!

Science is a study, a tool, a way and a means...it's global warming and Antarctic freezing. It's inside the body and outside the universe. Science is the key to the future. It's the answer to many problems. It's the cutting edge of the cutting edge!

If you don't learn science, you'll be in the dark. You'll also miss out on some amazing, fascinating, funny, mind-blowing, (NO lab-blowing, now—gotta promise!) facts, stories, experiments, and much more.

When you learn about science, you learn about yourself and your world. So JOIN THE SCIENCE ALLIANCE—and let's do science!

"I can't wait!"

Carole Marsh
Science Alliance Member Number 1

Nick navigates Natural Disasters!

Nick's Journal
Scientific Minds Camp—Day 1

Don't forget experiments start tomorrow!

Five minutes to "Lights Out!" I have to write fast! Today we saw a movie on natural disasters. It was pretty cool and kind of scary at the same time! Whole cities disappeared in floods, and erupting volcanoes caused mudslides miles wide!

I learned that some of the worst natural disasters in history happened right here in the United States. The San Francisco Fire of 1906 started out as a one-minute earthquake, and ended four days later! Gas lines broke and fires burned up the city!

Drought and heat are really bad things, too! In the summer of 1980, there was a terrible heat wave in the central and southern United States. Farmers had to leave their farms because of the drought! Lots of people died, too. Even though there is no way to prevent natural disasters from happening, scientists are getting smarter at finding ways to keep people safe.

We start our experiments tomorrow! We'll see how rain clouds form, and what makes lava move the way it does. I heard they have a wave pool to show us how avalanches can cause huge waves to form! Cool!

What is a Natural Disaster?

A **natural disaster** is an extreme (or very big!) event in nature that causes a lot of damage and hurts or kills many people or other living things.

Extremes of nature happen everywhere, in every corner of our planet. What are these extreme events? Some can be broken down like this: WINDY— blizzards, hurricanes, and tornadoes; WET—tsunamis and floods; HOT—wildfires and volcanoes. Droughts and earthquakes finish the list. They are normal parts of Earth's life cycles, but when they cause harm or destruction, we call them disasters.

The worst earthquake or hurricane you can imagine wouldn't be called a natural disaster if it happened where no one lived or could be hurt—let's say, in the middle of the ocean. The worst tornado wouldn't be a natural disaster if no buildings or bridges or other structures were damaged.

But the extreme forces of nature are very powerful and often hurt people and places. Communities can't prepare for all disasters, and man-made buildings and structures aren't strong enough to stand up to nature EVERY time.

Sharing Experiences

Interview 12 classmates. Find out who has experienced any of these extremes of nature firsthand. Color in one box for each "yes."

	1	2	3	4	5	6	7	8	9	10	11	12
Blizzard												
Earthquake												
Flood												
Drought												
Hurricane												
Tornado												
Wildfire												

I Think I'm Lost!

Have you ever been in a snowstorm? A really big snowstorm can turn into a blizzard!

So, what is a blizzard? A blizzard is a storm that lasts for at least three hours, has lots of wind (up to 35 miles per hour), and has blowing snow that makes it hard to see more than a quarter of a mile away.

What about temperature? You know that it has to be cold to snow. But even though temperature is important, it's not an "official" part of a blizzard.

Is it still called a blizzard if no snow is falling? Yes! If it's not snowing but snow is blowing around, it's called a ground blizzard. The wind just picks up the snow that has already fallen.

I've heard of whiteouts. Are they the same as blizzards? They are the worst kind of blizzards. So much snow is blowing around that you can't tell where the ground and the sky meet. Everything around you is white! Whiteouts are dangerous because they make you lose your sense of direction and you can get lost very easily.

Find Your Way!

Fill in the bubblegram with "blizzard" words! Use the letter clues to help you.

blizzard
temperature
snowstorm
whiteout
windy

1. ___ O I ___ ___ ___ U ___
2. ___ ___ ___ W ___ O ___ ___ ___
3. O ___ N ___ ___
4. ___ ___ O ___ ___ A ___ ___
5. ___ O ___ ___ E ___ ___ ___ ___ ___ E

Unscramble the bubble letters to fill in the missing word below.

When so much snow blows around that you can't tell up from down, everything around you looks ____________.

A Whole Lotta Shakin'

Everyone's heard of an **earthquake**, or when the earth shakes underneath you. Maybe you have seen the results of one—or even felt one yourself! But to understand what causes an earthquake, we have to look deep inside the earth, below the earth's crust, or top layer. What you'd see there would amaze you!

United States
North American Plate
Pacific Plate
San Francisco
San Andreas Fault
Los Angeles
Mexico

If you've ever put together a puzzle, you can picture what **tectonic plates** are. They are like giant puzzle pieces made of rock, forming a layer under the earth's crust. Just like in a puzzle, the pieces vary in shape and size.

The problem is, they move! They float on top of liquid rock like rafts on a lake. When the tectonic plates move, they create changes in pressure in the earth's crust above it, causing it to crack in certain places. These places are called **fault lines**.

Fault lines can be as small as a few millimeters or can run for many miles. The San Andreas fault line in California is over 600 miles long! It separates two tectonic plates, the North American Plate and the Pacific Plate. Some very big earthquakes have happened there.

Hold on tight!

Crack the Code

Use the code below to figure out the secret message!

Making Waves

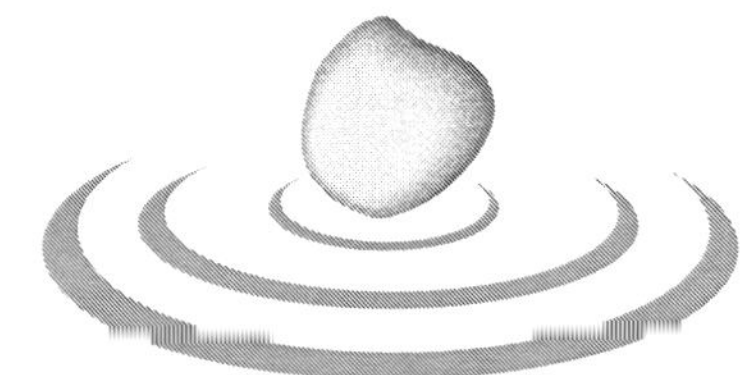

An earthquake starts at its **focus** inside the earth, sending out waves of energy called **seismic waves**. These waves form much like the ripples on water when you throw a pebble into a pond. They move differently according to their type.

P waves, or primary waves, move through solids (like rocks), liquids, and gases. They force rock particles to move backward and forward. This causes the back-and-forth motion during an earthquake.

S waves, or secondary waves, move through solids. They force rocks to move up and down and side to side, causing much damage to the Earth's crust. They produce the wave-like movements felt during an earthquake.

The **epicenter** is directly above the focus. This is where the most violent shaking on the surface happens. You don't want to be here during an earthquake!

An earthquake's **magnitude** tells you how strong the quake is by looking at the amount of energy it gives off. Magnitude is measured using the **Richter Scale**. An earthquake of magnitude 2 is the smallest that people can feel. The worst earthquakes usually measure 8 or higher, but even a 6 on the Richter Scale is very big!

Slinking Around!

Perform the experiment below to understand how earthquake waves behave.

Materials needed:
one Slinky® toy and one partner

Instructions:

1. Grab one end of the Slinky. Have your partner grab the other end and move six feet away from you.

2. Pull the Slinky toward you. Push it away. Watch the wave move from you to your partner. That is a P wave. P waves are the fastest earthquake waves.

3. Move your end of the Slinky up and down. Watch a different wave move along the Slinky. That is an S wave.

The word **tsunami** (soo NAH mee) means "harbor wave" in Japanese. Tsunamis are not tidal waves or wind-created waves. They are giant water waves caused by earthquakes, volcanic eruptions, and landslides or meteorites that fall into the sea. These events displace or move the water very quickly—much like water splashes out of your glass if you drop in too many ice cubes!

Out at sea, tsunami waves are usually smaller than three feet. Even fishermen don't see them! In fact, when a tsunami is coming at the shore, out at sea is the safest place to be. On shore, ten-story waves can reach a mile inland, flooding everything in the way.

Tsunami waves move faster in deep water. In 15,000 feet of water, a wave travels nearly 500 miles an hour, crossing the ocean at the speed of a jet airplane!

Most tsunamis hit shores near where they are made. But the Sumatra tsunami that struck on December 26, 2004, hit 18 Indian Ocean countries. It killed nearly 300,000 people and caused damage in countries as far away as South Africa and Australia.

Puzzle Time!

Find the following words in the word search below.

WORD BANK

flood
earthquakes
faster
water
safest
jet
mile
tsunami

N	U	W	A	T	E	R	R	Q	K	L	M
J	U	P	G	Y	A	Y	T	G	W	P	T
S	C	G	Z	N	R	O	I	M	E	J	Z
T	T	C	T	R	T	R	E	T	S	A	F
K	D	S	S	U	H	K	J	P	N	G	C
D	E	Z	E	O	Q	A	R	Q	D	E	T
O	Y	L	Y	F	U	Q	J	M	L	S	E
O	W	T	E	R	A	H	Q	I	U	K	Q
L	G	Z	V	B	K	S	M	N	M	K	O
F	J	C	V	C	E	M	A	M	J	Q	N
W	A	E	E	Q	S	M	O	H	A	N	S
I	J	R	T	L	I	H	B	V	L	A	T

Soaked to the Bone

Have you ever watered a plant so much that the water ran over the sides of the flower pot? It's like a mini flood! A **flood** is when bodies of water, such as rivers and lakes, rise and overflow.

Heavy rainstorms are a major cause of flooding. When it rains too much, the ground gets **saturated**. This means the soil can't hold any more water, just like the dirt in your flower pot couldn't. The extra rain runs into lakes and ponds. Then there is nowhere else for water to go—but up!

Do you know why it rains? As temperatures get hotter, liquid water turns to gas and rises. This is **evaporation**. As this gas, or **vapor,** rises, it cools and forms clouds. This is **condensation**. A hot day may feel **humid**, or sort of damp. That's because water is evaporating from everywhere—sidewalks, grass, and lakes. What you feel is water vapor.

When water droplets in the clouds touch each other, they join to make bigger drops. The droplets get heavier and heavier. Then gravity pulls them down to the ground as **rain**!

Water Works

Try this experiment to see how evaporation and condensation work.

Materials needed:

- 4 cups of dirt or sand
- 12 rocks
- 2 quarts of water
- 1 large, glass bowl with tall sides
- 1 short, empty glass
- clear plastic wrap
- a sunny day

Instructions:

1. Mix the dirt (or sand) and the water in the large, glass bowl.

2. Put the short, empty glass in the center of the bowl.

3. Put the bowl outside in the sun.

4. Cover the bowl with plastic wrap. Weigh down the edges with all but one of the rocks. Place the last rock on the plastic wrap, directly over the short, empty glass.

3. Keep the bowl in the sun for several hours. Then check the small glass. What do you see in the glass? What do you see in the large bowl? Where did water evaporate? Where did it condense?

Whew, It's Dry!

Dear Journal,

When I got home from school, Mom was watching the weather report on TV. I heard the word drought a lot (it sounds like "shout") and that surprised me. I know it means that the land and air have been too dry for a long time, but I thought that only happened in countries like Africa!

When I took out the trash, I noticed that Mom's garden was dying. I asked her why, and she said there are water restrictions now, so she can't water at all. I have to take shorter showers now. And when I'm done, instead of throwing my towel in the laundry room, I have to hang it up to use it again.

Then we went to the park. I can't believe the pond in the middle of the park has almost completely dried up! Mom told me that water is evaporating at a faster rate than it's precipitating, or raining down. She said it was due to the unusually dry weather all season long. That's why we have to conserve, or be careful not to use too much water.

All Dried Up?

Using the word bank, solve the crossword puzzle below.

Word Bank

drought
evaporating
precipitating
water restrictions
conserve

Across

1. water falling from the sky
3. limits on water use
4. dryness lasting a long time
5. water turning into a gas, or vapor

Down

2. to use up less of a resource like water

Fast and Furious

About five hurricanes hit the U.S. coastline (from Texas to Maine) over every three-year period. Of those five, about two are very destructive!

A **hurricane** is a storm that has steady winds of at least 74 miles per hour (that's how fast your car goes on the highway!) and typically extends about 300 miles wide. Hurricanes form over very warm water—80 degrees or warmer.

Hurricanes, also known as typhoons and cyclones, form near the equator. The earth's rotation helps start the spinning motion of hurricanes. This is called the **Coriolis effect**. Storms that form north of the equator spin counterclockwise. Storms south of the equator spin clockwise.

Hurricane winds cause the sea to rise and huge waves to form. Throw in heavy rains from the storms, and you have a recipe for flooding. Hurricanes eventually die as they move across land, but not before they've caused much damage to the coastline.

Let's Spin!

Try this experiment to see how the earth's rotation causes the Coriolis effect.

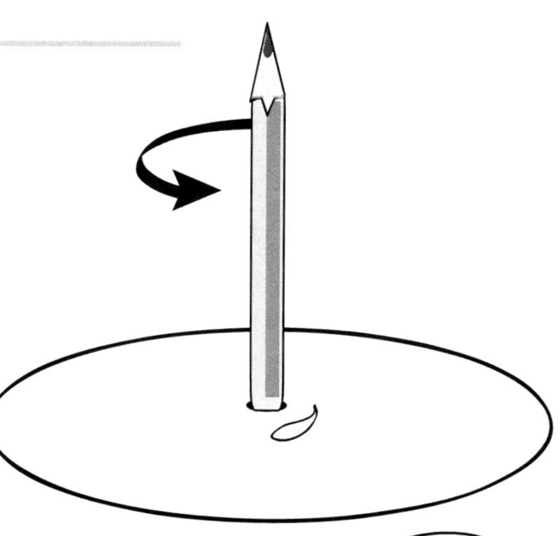

Materials needed: Thick paper (at least 8 inches wide), scissors, a pencil, and an eyedropper

Instructions:

1. Cut an 8-inch wide circle out of the thick paper. Push the pencil through the center of the circle. Hold the pencil up and down, so the paper is horizontal, or flat.

2. Put a drop of water on the paper near the center of the circle. Twirl the pencil between your hands in a counter-clockwise direction (pull your left hand toward you). What happens to the water drop?

Twisting in the Wind

Hi, I'm Tori the Tornado! I'm here to tell you all about me and my "whirling, twirling" friends!

Tornadoes, sometimes called **twisters**, are very violent forces of nature. We are spinning columns of air that drop and hang from thunderstorms. We weave back and forth, turning with ferocious speeds—up to 300 miles an hour! We can fling trucks through the air, uproot trees, and knock down buildings.

I know I have a bad reputation for destroying everything in my path. But did you know that I can't appear whenever I want to? Just the right ingredients are needed to make me:

Parent Thunderstorm: Take warm, wet air near the ground and shove it up into thick, colder air. This will make a nice thunderstorm.

Wind Shear: Change the wind speed and the direction of the wind as the warm air moves up. This will get a great spin in motion.

Unstable Atmosphere: Put a layer of hot, dry air between the warm air beneath and the cold air above. This will make the warm air on the bottom get even warmer and cause the atmosphere to be really unstable, or quick to change—perfect conditions for me, Tori!

Storm Central

What do, Iowa, Kansas, Nebraska, Oklahoma, and Texas have in common? They are part of an area of the United States known as **Tornado Alley**. That's where I like to hang out! This region has lots of tornadoes every year! Remember, though, tornadoes can form anywhere.

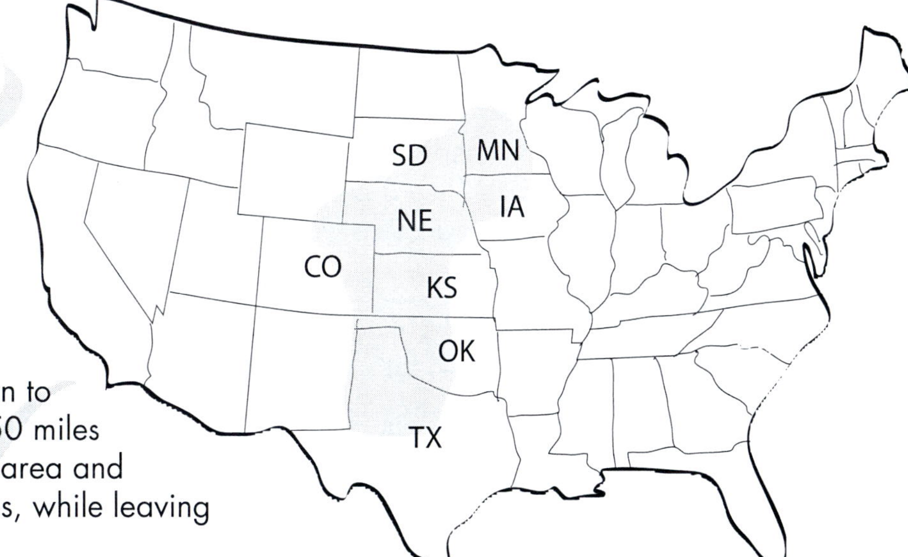

Tornadoes form year-round, but we tend to start popping up around the beginning of spring in March, when there is lots of warm, humid air. Tornado season usually ends in August.

My friends and I have been known to damage areas one mile wide and 50 miles long. Sometimes I pass through an area and completely knock down some houses, while leaving others without a scratch!

Damage Control

Scientists like to measure me! The force of a tornado is measured by the **Fujita Tornado Damage Scale**. The Fujita Scale is based on the amount of damage a tornado causes and ranges from EF0 (least damage) to EF5 (most damage).

For example, an EF0 tornado can break tree branches and rip down signs. An EF3 can throw around cars and blow roofs off of houses. An EF5 can sweep away entire buildings and tear bark right off the trees! There are some mean tornadoes out there!

Tornado True or False

Read the sentences below. Circle True or False.

1. TRUE / FALSE A tornado drops from a thunderstorm.
2. TRUE / FALSE Tornadoes can reach temperatures of 300 degrees.
3. TRUE / FALSE Wind shear describes how winds suddenly change.
4. TRUE / FALSE California is in Tornado Alley.
5. TRUE / FALSE Tornadoes can form at any time of year.
6. TRUE / FALSE The Fujita Scale is based on how much damage a tornado can do.
7. TRUE / FALSE Tornadoes aren't strong enough to knock down buildings.

When you think of a **volcano**, you probably think of a mountain with hot, molten (melted) rock and ash pouring out of its top. This kind of volcano is called a stratovolcano.

Stratovolcanoes erupt when pressure moves molten rock, or **magma**, up from deep in the earth through a **vent**, which acts like a pipe. The vent opens into a bowl-shaped crater at the top of the mountain. As the magma makes its way up through the layers of earth, it pushes solid rock out of its way.

The magma comes out of the mountain (now it's called **lava**) with a big explosion of rock, gases, and ash that can travel for miles! As the lava hardens, it forms new layers of the mountain.

Not all volcanoes are active. Active volcanoes are ones that have erupted recently or might erupt at any time. Dormant, or sleeping, volcanoes can stay quiet for hundreds of years! Either they have a hardened lava plug or their magma has moved back down under the earth's crust.

Magmatic Matching!

Match the volcanic terms to the volcano diagram.

1. ______ Lava flow
2. ______ Layer of hardened lava
3. ______ Ash cloud
4. ______ Crater
5. ______ Vent
6. ______ Magma

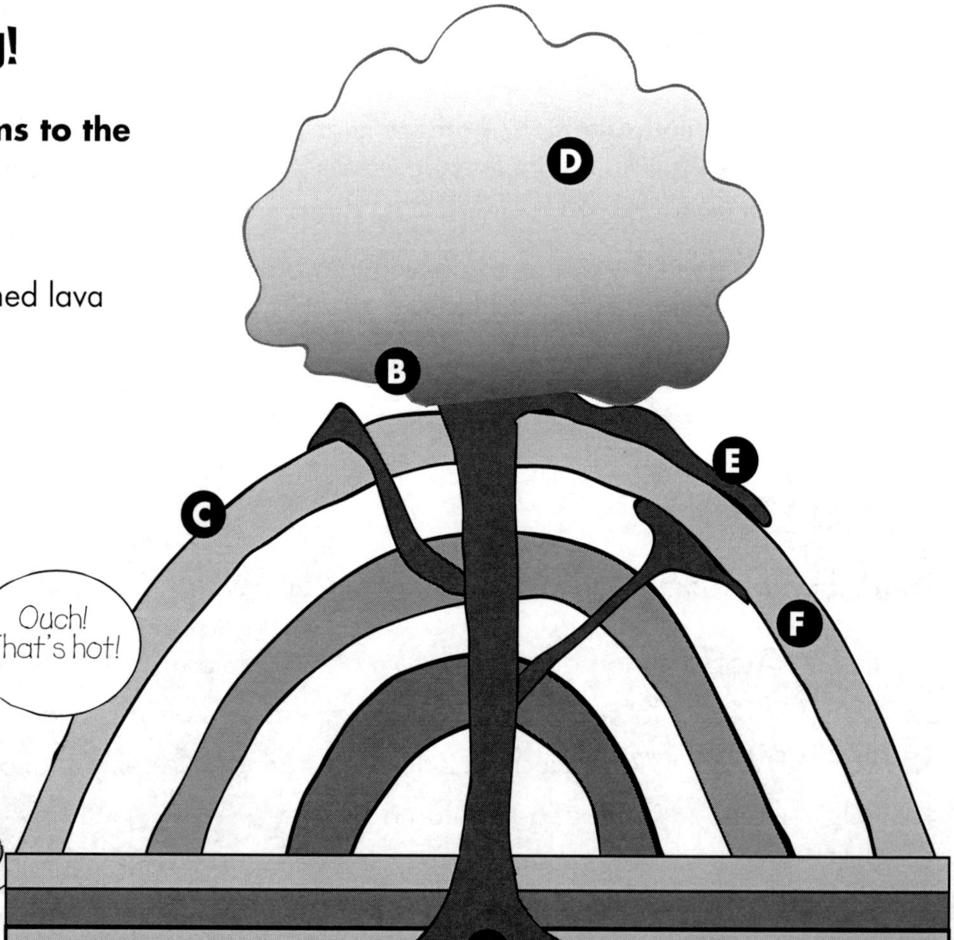

D
B
E
C
F
A

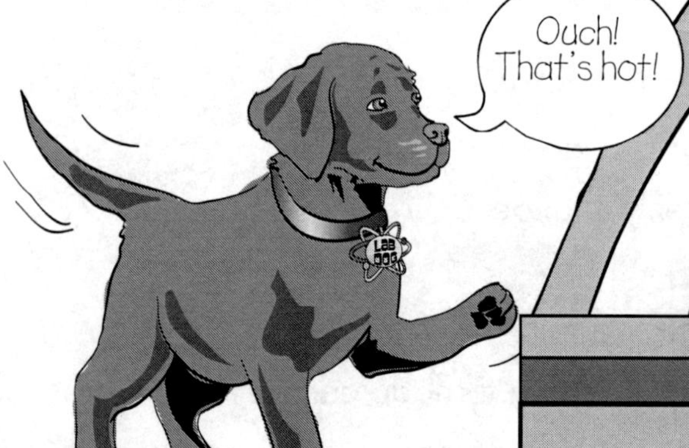

Ouch! That's hot!

Go With the Flow!

Molten rock released from a volcano is called **lava**. Lava is extremely hot with temperatures between 700 and 1,200 degrees. (Watch your toes!) Lava isn't always red. Depending on the temperature, it might be orange, yellow, or even white. The lighter the color, the hotter it is! (Maybe that's where the term "white-hot" came from!)

Once lava stops moving, it is cool enough within ten minutes for you to step on it. But—your shoes might melt! (Try explaining that one to your mom!)

While it is underground, molten rock is called **magma**. Other than being a little cooler, there is very little difference between magma and lava. Lava can shoot out of the ground in amazing fountains up to 2,000 feet high. (Don't stick around to watch, though!) Usually, lava moves very slowly down the side of a volcano. The temperature of the lava affects its flow rate—the hotter the lava, the faster it flows!

Let's Watch the Flow!

Perform the experiment below to see how lava flows.

Materials needed:

raised relief map (area like the Hawaiian Islands)
several plastic drinking straws
one jar of molasses

Instructions:

1. Place the map on the floor.

2. Dip the straw in the molasses. Put your finger over the top to keep the molasses inside the straw.

3. Keeping your finger in place, move the straw to the top of a mountain (or volcano) on the relief map.

4. Remove your finger from the top of the straw, releasing the "lava" onto the mountainside. Gravity will pull the "lava" down the side of the mountain.

5. Try it again on a steeper mountain. Did the molasses move faster or slower?

6. Try guessing how much molasses you would need to get your lava to flow to a certain point on your map. (Keep your fingers out of the molasses—it's very sticky!)

Where There's Smoke . . .

A **wildfire** is a fire that happens in a wilderness area, such as a forest, or in rural areas, such as the plains. Wildfires can be started by people or by natural forces, like lightning and lava. Earthquakes can sometimes cause one.

Wildfires are very common during times of drought, when trees and grasses are extra dry. But it's not always the dry stuff that burns. A wet bale of hay can make enough heat from organisms growing inside it to burst into flame! As long as there is heat, a fire can start.

Wind makes fires spread and can carry them into developed areas, or places where people live. This threatens lives and buildings.

Crawling fires spread along low-lying bushes. **Crown fires** move along the top branches of trees and spread really fast! They create their own wind by pulling in air from around them. It is very hard to outrun a crown fire. **Jumping fires** are carried by the wind when burning leaves and branches break loose. This type of fire is hard to control. You don't know where it's going next!

...There's FIRE

Using the information above, fill in the blanks.

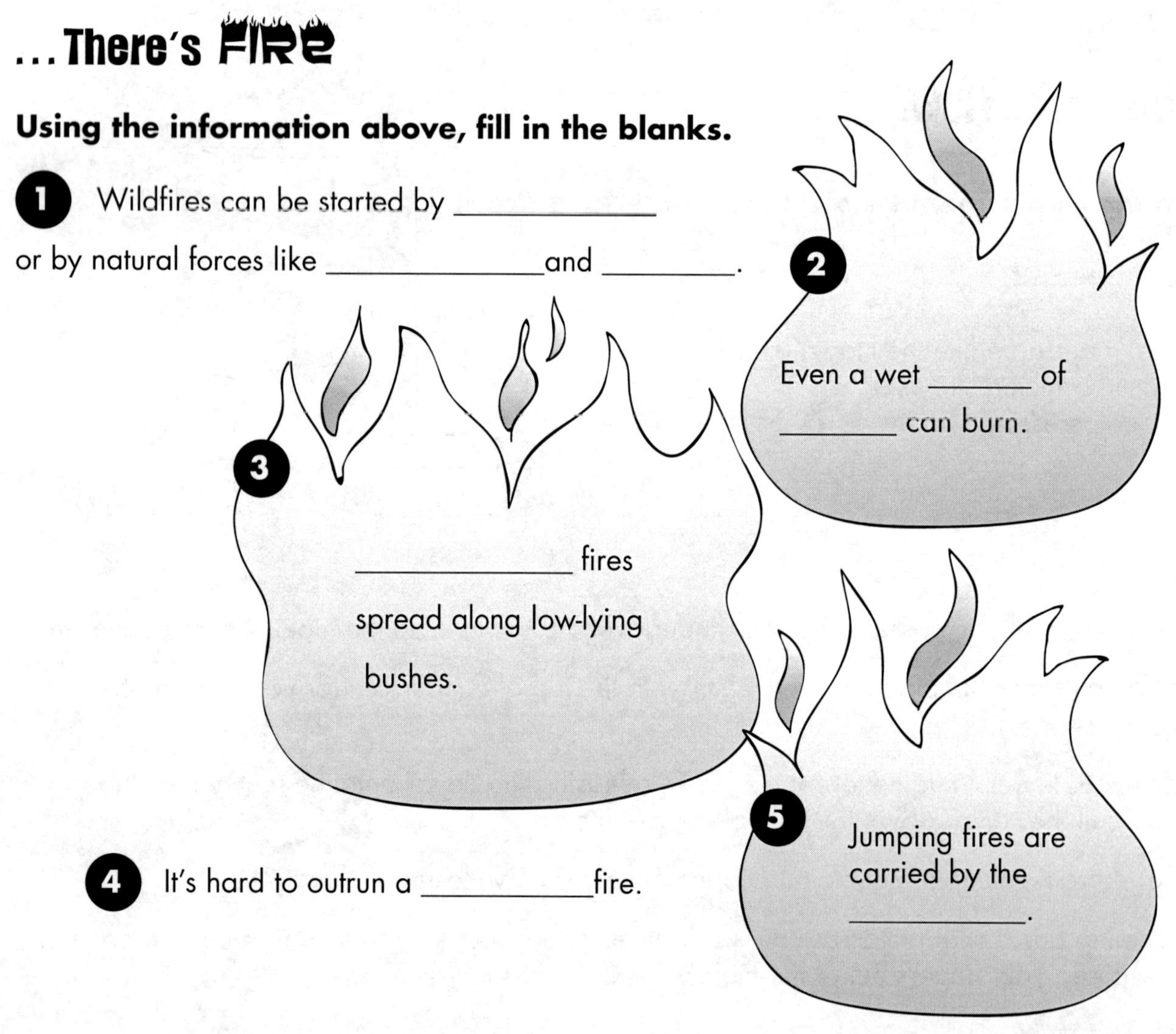

1. Wildfires can be started by ____________ or by natural forces like ____________ and ________.

2. Even a wet ______ of _______ can burn.

3. ____________ fires spread along low-lying bushes.

4. It's hard to outrun a ___________ fire.

5. Jumping fires are carried by the ___________.

Studying natural disasters requires special tools and equipment. Some of them are listed below.

Earthquakes

- **Seismographs** are instruments that measure and record the magnitude of an earthquake.
- The **Richter Scale** rates the strength of an earthquake, using a scale from 1 to 10.

Volcanoes

- An **electronic tiltmeter** measures slight tilts in the land near a volcano, which indicate that magma is rising and falling.

Drought

- The **Palmer Index** is a scale that measures the level of moisture in the soil.

Tornadoes, Hurricanes, Storms

- The **Fujita Scale** rates tornadoes by the amount of damage they do.
- **Doppler Radar** measures wind direction and speed and can indicate how big hail is and how much rain is falling. It lets forecasters "see" severe thunderstorms that may bring wind, hail, heavy rain, and tornadoes.
- **Satellites** allow a bird's-eye view of developing storm systems.
- The **Saffir-Simpson Hurricane Scale** rates hurricanes based on wind speeds, flooding, and damage. Category 1 is the weakest and Category 5 is the strongest.
- **Weather balloons** carry equipment that measures pressure, temperature, and humidity in the atmosphere.

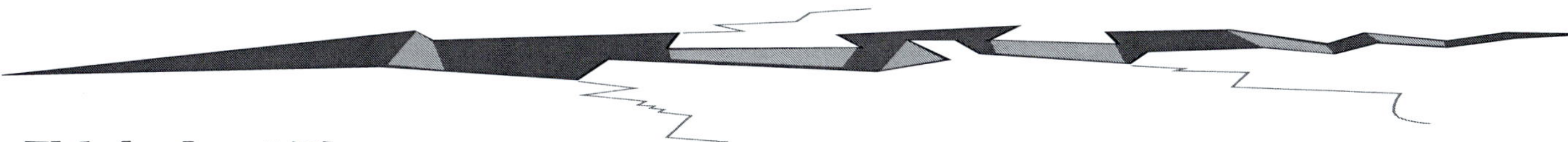

Think about It!

Fill in the blanks below.

1. Which tool can be used by weather forecasters for hurricanes, tornadoes, thunderstorms, and other storms?

_______________ _______________

2. Which tool rates the strength of an earthquake?

_______________ _______________

3. Which tool rates the strength of a tornado?

_______________ _______________

There are many jobs that study, predict, and respond to natural disasters. Here are just a few:

Seismologists are earth scientists who study earthquakes and use special equipment to measure and detect earthquakes.

Meteorologists study and forecast the weather, including severe storms.

Volcanologists study volcanoes and signs of volcanic activity. They warn people and cities when a volcano may erupt, and therefore save many lives.

Firefighters put out fires and give emergency medical treatment. Some firefighters work only with forest fires. Smoke jumpers are forest-fire fighters who parachute from airplanes to reach fires in out-of-the-way places.

Humanitarian workers help people and places recover after a natural disaster.

What do you like?

Which career appeals to you? ______________________________

Why? ____

Will give love for food.

____

____

Have you ever thought about being an inventor? Have you watched a show on TV where someone showed his invention to the world? How can you become an inventor?

All of us create or invent something at some time in our lives. Usually, it's something we use to fix a problem. However, for you to achieve the status of a "true inventor," you must be able to go beyond the ordinary!

Did you know that not all scientists graduated from college? Some, like Thomas Edison, didn't even go to school. They taught themselves by reading everything they could on subjects they liked. There are certain attributes that make a person successful. Do you know what those attributes are?

The Right Stuff!

Circle the following words that play an important role in achieving success.

PATIENCE WISDOM

MISTAKES FAILURE LAZINESS

ENCOURAGEMENT

PERSEVERANCE GIVING UP

TIME EXCUSES WHINING

OPTIMISM BRAINSTORMING

Seismologist **Charles F. Richter** developed the Richter magnitude scale to measure the size and strength of earthquakes.

Alfred Wegener was a meteorologist who theorized that the continents were moving apart. He called it continental drift. He also created the first weather balloons.

Meteorologist **Jule Charney** is considered the father of numerical weather prediction. Through his work, scientists understand more about weather forecasting.

Maurice and Katia Krafft were famous volcanologists who studied and videotaped active volcanoes. Their films showed how dangerous volcanoes could be and why people should leave the area before an eruption.

Who Did What?

Draw a line to match the scientists below with their discoveries.

A. John Tuzo Wilson

B. Charles F. Richter

C. Alfred Wegener

D. Jule Charney

E. Maurice and Katia Krafft

1. 

2. WEATHER

3. 

4. 

5. 

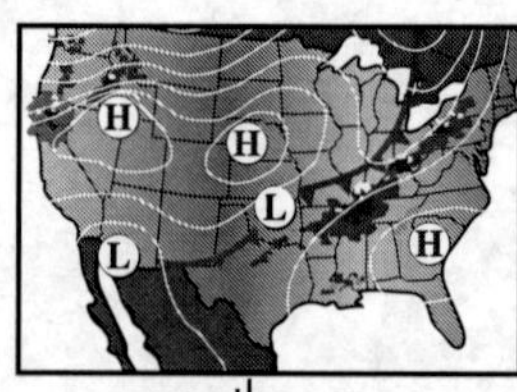

weather map

The Scientific Method

Scientists use the scientific method to explore observations and answer questions about why something happens the way it does. They make a prediction about something and then design experiments to prove or disprove their idea, or **hypothesis**.

To make the scientific method work for you, follow the steps below to construct a hypothesis, design an experiment, and to perform and evaluate your experiment. Just like for a scientist, the scientific method helps you focus your questions about your idea. When you consistently get the same results from your experiments, your hypothesis becomes a **theory**. A theory is an idea or belief about something you've arrived at through experimentation.

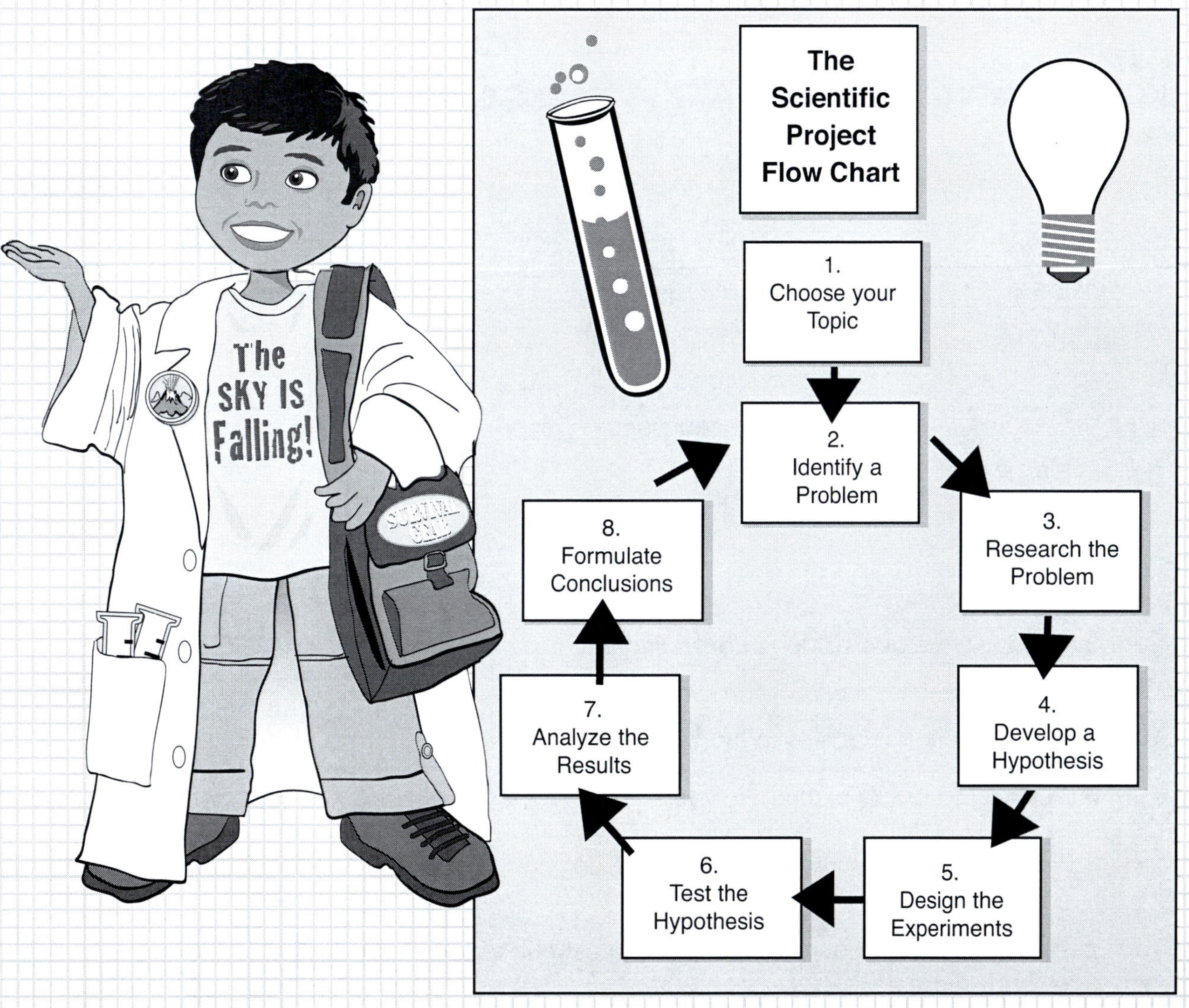

How Does a Seismograph Record Earthquake Activity?

Background:

An earthquake shakes the ground with violent energy. Scientists use seismographs to record the magnitude, or the shaking energy, of an earthquake.

Objective:

The objective of this project is to see how a seismograph records the magnitude of an earthquake.

Materials:

- a cardboard box (12" x 12" is best) with one side open
- scissors
- ruler
- adding-machine paper
- a 5-ounce paper cup
- masking tape
- black marking pen
- 5 ounces of small rocks
- sharpened pencil
- string

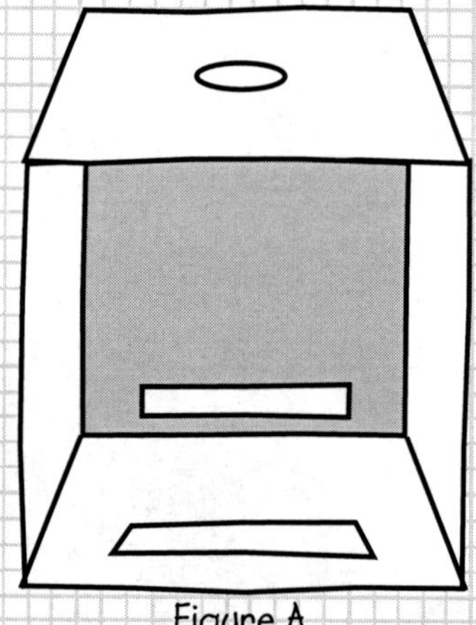

Figure A

Methods:

1. Prepare the box as follows:
   a. Turn the box, so the open side is not facing up, but out.
   b. Cut a 2-inch hole in the center of the top of the box.
   c. Cut two 1/2-inch x 4-inch slits in the box (see Figure A).
2. Cut a 24-inch strip of adding-machine paper.
3. Thread the strip of paper through the slits in the box (see Figure B).
4. Use your pencil or scissors to punch two small holes in the cup, one on each side, near the rim.
5. Cut two 18-inch pieces of string. Tie each string to one side of the cup, through the holes near the rim.

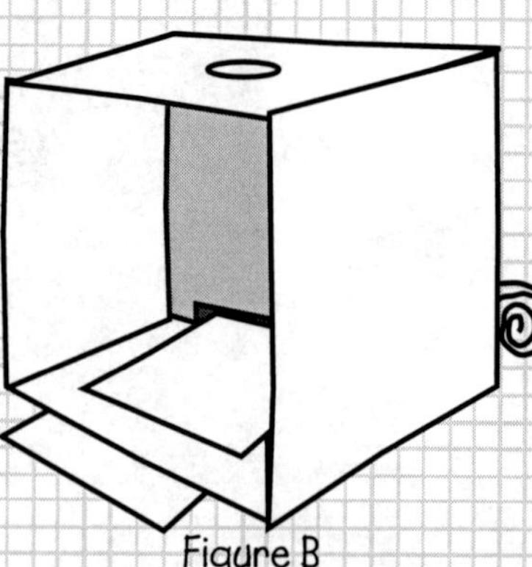

Figure B

6. Set the cup in the box. Thread the loose ends of the strings up and out of the 2-inch hole in the top of the box.

7. Tape the loose ends of the strings to the middle of the pencil. Lay the pencil on top of the box. Wind up the strings until the bottom of the cup is 1 inch from the bottom of the box. Tape down the two ends of the pencil to the top of the box.

8. Push the black marking pen down through the bottom of the cup, so that the tip of the pen touches the paper below it. Fill the cup with small rocks to surround the pen.

Results:

1. Pull the adding-machine paper toward you as you gently shake the box with your other hand. Report the results in the chart below.

2. Continue to pull the adding machine paper toward you. Shake the box with a little more force. Report the results.

3. Add more rocks to your cup. Use gentle shakes as in Step 1. Does this affect the results? Report the results.

4. Remove all of the rocks from the cup. Use gentle shakes as in Step 1. Does this affect the results? Report the results.

5. What if you vary the direction of the shaking? North, south, east, west? Determine where north and south are. Move the box back and forth in those directions, using gentle shakes as in Step 1. Report the results. Repeat with east and west.

Variations	Seismogram Results
Few Rocks	
More Force	
More rocks	
No rocks	
North	
South	
East	
West	

6. Turn to page 28 and answer the questions.

Wow! Look at that!

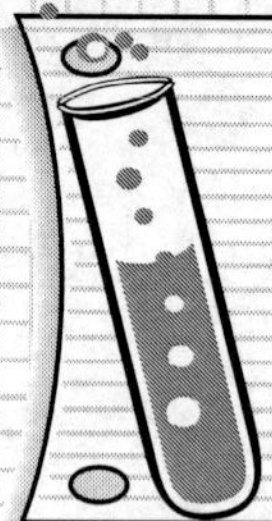

What Did I Learn?

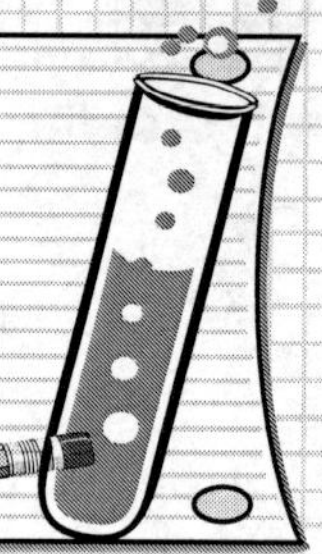

Here's your chance to describe what you learned in your science fair experiment!

1. When I started my project, what was I trying to find out?

____

____

____

2. What were my actual results?

____

____

____

3. Did my research method give me quality results? Why or why not?

____

____

____

4. What would I do differently if I did this project again?

____

____

____

Join the Science Alliance

Join the Science Alliance by raising your right hand and saying the pledge below.

Science Alliance Pledge:

I, ______________________, agree to pay attention to... learn about... learn to love... learn to use... learn to share... good science in school and my daily life so that others and I may benefit from more knowledge and skill in this important subject. I also agree to accept the idea that it is better to have knowledge and never need to use it, than to not have knowledge and need to use it.

____

Sign your name here.

Sam
Molly
Ellie
Lara
Steven
Eddie
Willie
Mandy

Robby
Fred
Hannah
Gina
Luke
Nick
Christina
Nina

Metric Conversions

Conversions To Metric Measures

Symbol	When You Know	Multiply By	To Find	Symbol
		LENGTH		
in	inches	25.4	millimeters	mm
ft	feet	0.305	meters	m
yd	yards	0.914	meters	m
mi	miles	1.61	kilometers	km
		AREA		
in^2	square inches	645.2	square millimeters	mm^2
ft^2	square feet	0.093	square meters	m^2
yd^2	square yard	0.836	square meters	m^2
ac	acres	0.405	hectares	ha
mi^2	square miles	2.59	square kilometers	km^2
		VOLUME		
fl oz	fluid ounces	29.57	milliliters	mL
gal	gallons	3.785	liters	L
ft^3	cubic feet	0.028	cubic meters	m^3
yd^3	cubic yards	0.765	cubic meters	m^3
		MASS		
oz	ounces	28.35	grams	g
lb	pounds	0.454	kilograms	kg
T	short tons (2000 lb)	0.907	megagrams (or "metric ton")	Mg (or "t")
		TEMPERATURE		
°F	Fahrenheit	1. Subtract 32 from Fahrenheit number 2. Multiply answer by 5 3. Divide answer by 9	Celsius	°C

Glossary

blizzard: strong winds in snowy conditions that last three hours and make visibility difficult

condensation: the process where a gas cools and becomes a liquid

drought: extreme dryness or unusual lack of precipitation for at least a season

earthquake: the result of a sudden release of energy in the earth's crust, resulting in seismic waves

epicenter: the point directly above the focus, or starting point, of an earthquake

evaporation: the process where a liquid heats up and turns to a gas

fault line: where the earth's crust is vulnerable to earthquakes and volcanoes

ground blizzard: storm that meets blizzard conditions with no snow falling

hurricane: tropical storm with sustained winds of at least 74 miles per hour and a wide base

magma: melted rock in the core of the earth—it is called lava when it comes out of a volcano

seismic waves: energy waves given off during earthquakes that result in the ground shaking

tectonic plates: rock slabs under the earth's crust that collide, move apart, or grate against each other, causing earthquakes and volcanoes

tornadoes: rotating columns of air with speeds of up to 300 miles per hour

tsunami: giant waves caused by a sudden displacement of water

volcano: expels hot, molten lava from the center of the earth

wildfire: uncontrolled fire in wilderness or rural areas

Answer Key

Page 9
1. whiteout; 2. snowstorm; 3. windy;
4. blizzard; 5. temperature; Bubble word: white

Page 10
I feel the earth move!

Page 12

N	U	W	A	T	E	R	R	Q	K	L	M
J	U	P	G	Y	A	Y	T	G	W	P	T
S	C	G	Z	N	R	O	I	M	E	J	Z
T	T	C	T	R	T	R	E	T	S	A	F
K	D	S	S	U	H	K	J	P	N	G	C
D	E	Z	E	O	Q	A	R	Q	D	E	T
O	Y	L	Y	F	U	Q	J	M	L	S	E
O	W	T	E	R	A	H	Q	I	U	K	Q
L	G	Z	V	B	K	S	M	N	M	K	O
F	J	C	V	C	E	M	A	M	J	Q	N
W	A	E	E	Q	S	M	O	H	A	N	S
I	J	R	T	L	I	H	B	V	L	A	T

Page 14

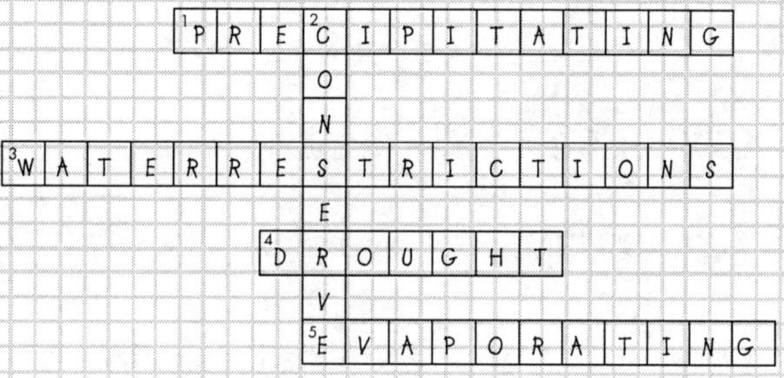

Page 17
1. True; 2. False; 3. True; 4. False; 5. True; 6. True; 7. False

Page 18
1. E; 2. F; 3. D; 4. C; 5. B; 6. A

Page 20
1. people, lightning, lava; 2. bale, hay; 3. Crawling; 4. crown; 5. wind

Page 21
1. Doppler Radar; 2. Richter Scale; 3. Fujita Scale

Page 23
patience, wisdom, mistakes, failure, encouragement, perseverance, time, optimism, brainstorming

Page 24
A. 3; B. 4; C. 2; D. 5; E. 1